D1106481

Modern Man Is Obsolete

Modern Man Is Obsolete

Norman Cousins

THE VIKING PRESS · NEW YORK
1945

Published by The Viking Press in October 1945

Published on the same day in the Dominion of Canada
by the Macmillan Company of Canada Limited

Second Printing October 1945

Printed in U.S.A.
by H. Wolff Book Manufacturing Company

Contents

Modern Man Is Obsolete

THE BEGINNING of the Atomic Age has brought less hope than fear. It is a primitive fear, the fear of the unknown, the fear of forces man can neither channel nor comprehend. This fear is not new; in its classical form it is the fear of irrational death. But overnight it has become intensified, magnified. It has burst out of the subconscious and into the conscious, filling the mind with primordial apprehensions. It is thus that man stumbles fitfully into a new era of atomic energy for which he is as ill equipped to accept its potential blessings as he is to control its present dangers.

Where man can find no answer, he will find fear. While the dust was still settling over Hiroshima, he was asking himself questions and finding no answers. The biggest question of these concerns himself. Is war inevitable because it is in the nature of man? If so, how much time has he left—five, ten, twenty years—before he employs the means now available to him for the ultimate in self-destruction—extinction? If not, then how is he to interpret his own experience, which tells him that in all recorded history there have been only three hundred years in the aggregate during which he was free of war?

Clearly following upon these are other questions, flowing out endlessly from his fears and without prospect of definitive answer. Even assuming that he could hold destructive science in check, what changes would the new age bring or demand in his everyday life? What changes would it bring or demand in his culture, his education, his philosophy, his religion, his relationships with other human beings?

In speculating upon these questions, it should not be necessary to prove that on August 6, 1945, a new age was born. When on that day a parachute containing a small object floated to earth over Japan, it marked the violent death of one stage in man's history and the beginning of another. Nor should it be necessary to prove the saturating effect of the new age, permeating every aspect of man's activities, from machines to morals, from physics to philosophy, from politics to poetry; in sum, an effect creating a blanket of obsolescence not only over the methods and the products of man but over man himself.

It is a curious phenomenon of nature that only two species practice the art of war—men and ants, both of which, significantly, maintain complex social organizations. This does not mean that only men and ants engage in the murder of their own kind. Many animals of the same species kill each other, but only men and ants have practiced the science of organized destruction, employing their massed numbers in violent combat and relying on strategy and tactics to meet developing situations or to capitalize on the weaknesses in the strategy and tactics of the other side. The longest continuous war ever fought between men lasted thirty years. The longest ant war ever recorded lasted six-and-a-half weeks, or whatever the corresponding units would be in ant reckoning.

While all entomologists are agreed that war is instinctive with ants, it is encouraging to note that not all anthropologists and biologists are agreed that war is instinctive with men. Those who lean on experience, of course, find everything in man's history to indicate that war is locked up within his nature. But a broader and more generous, certainly more philosophical, view is held by those scientists who claim that the evidence of a war instinct in men is incomplete and misleading, and that man *does* have within him the power of abolishing war. Julian Huxley, the English biologist, draws a sharp distinction between human nature and the *expression* of human nature. Thus war is not a reflection but an expression of man's nature. Moreover, the expression may change, as the factors which lead to war may change. "In man, as in ants, war in any serious sense is bound up with the existence of accumulations of property to fight about. . . . As for human nature, it contains no specific war instinct, as does the nature of harvester ants. There is in man's makeup a general aggressive tendency, but this, like all other human urges, is not a specific and unvarying instinct; it can be molded into the most varied forms."

But even if this gives us a reassuring answer to the question—is war inevitable because of man's nature?—it still leaves unanswered the question concerning the causes leading up to war. The expression of man's nature will continue to be warlike if the same conditions are continued that have provoked warlike expressions in him in the past. And since man's sur-

---

Man is but a reed, the most feeble thing in nature, but he is a thinking reed. The entire universe need not arm itself to crush him. A vapor, a drop of water suffices to kill him. . . . All our dignity, then, consists of thought. By it we must elevate ourselves, and not by space and time which we cannot fill. Let us endeavor then to think well: that is the principle of morality. By space the universe encompasses and swallows me up like an atom; by thought I comprehend the world.

—Blaise Pascal, "The Philosophers" (1670)

---

vival on earth is now absolutely dependent on his ability to avoid a new war, he is faced with the so-far insoluble problem of eliminating those causes.

In the most primitive sense, war in man is an expression of his extreme competitive impulses. Like everything else in nature, he has had to fight for existence; but the battle against other animals, once won, gave way in his evolution to battle against his own kind. Darwin called it natural selection; Spencer called it the survival of the fittest; and its most overstretched interpretation is to be found in *Mein Kampf*, with the naked glorification of brute force and the complete worship of might makes right. In the political and national sense, it has been the attempt of the "have-nots" to take from the "haves," or the attempt of the "haves" to add further to their lot at the expense of the "have-nots." Not always was property at stake; comparative advantages were measured in terms of power, and in terms of tribal or national superiority. The good luck of one nation became the hard luck of another.

◇◇

Let Earth unbalanced from her orbit fly,
Planets and Suns run lawless through the sky;
Let ruling angels from their spheres be hurled,
Beings on Beings wrecked, and world on world . . .
So, wondrous creature, mount where Science guides;
Go, measure Earth, weigh air, and state the tides;
Instruct the planets in what orbs to run,
Correct old Time, and regulate the Sun . . .

* * *

Atoms or systems into ruin hurled,
And now a bubble burst, and now a world.

—Alexander Pope, "An Essay on Man" (1733)

◇◇

The good fortune of the Western powers in obtaining "concessions" in China at the turn of the century was the ill fortune of the Chinese. The power that Germany stripped from Austria, Czechoslovakia, Poland, and France at the beginning of World War II she added to her own.

What does it matter, then, if war is not in the nature of man so long as man continues through the expression of his nature to be a viciously competitive animal? The effect is the same, and therefore the result must be as conclusive—war being the effect, and complete obliteration of the human species being the ultimate result.

If this reasoning is correct, then modern man is obsolete, a self-made anachronism becoming more incongruous by the minute. He has exalted change in everything but himself. He has leaped centuries ahead in inventing a new world to live in, but he knows little or nothing about his own part in that world. He has surrounded and confounded himself with gaps—gaps between revolutionary technology and evolutionary man, between cosmic gadgets and human wisdom, between intellect and conscience. The struggle between science and morals that Henry Thomas Buckle foresaw a century ago has been all but won by science.

Given ample time, man might be expected eventually to span those gaps normally; but by his own hand, he is destroying even time. Decision and execution in the modern world are becoming virtually synchronous. Thus, whatever gaps man has to span he will have to span immediately.

This involves both biology and will. If he lacks the actual and potential biological equipment to build those bridges,

◇◇

No man can rob us of our will.

—EPICTETUS (c. 60)

◇◇

then the birth certificate of the atomic age is in reality a *memento mori.* But even if he possesses the necessary biological equipment, he must still make the decision which says that he is to apply himself to the challenge. Capability without decision is inaction and inconsequence.

MAN IS left, then, with a crisis in decision. The main test before him involves his *will* to change rather than his *ability* to change. That he is capable of change is certain. For there is no more mutable or adaptable animal in the world. We have seen him migrate from one extreme clime to another. We have seen him step out of backward societies and join advanced groups within the space of a single generation. This is not to imply that the changes were necessarily always for the better; only that change was and is possible. But change requires stimulus; and mankind today need look no further for stimulus than its own desire to stay alive. The critical power of change, says Spengler, is directly linked to the survival drive. Once the instinct for survival is stimulated, the basic condition for change can be met.

That is why the power of total destruction as potentially represented by modern science must be dramatized and kept in the forefront of public opinion. The full dimensions of the peril must be seen and recognized. Only then will man realize that the first order of business is the question of continued existence. Only then will he be prepared to make the decisions necessary to assure that survival.

IN MAKING these decisions, two principal courses are open to him. Both will keep him alive for an indefinite or at least a reasonably long period. These courses, however, are directly contradictory and represent polar extremes of approach.

The first course is the positive approach. It begins with a

careful survey and appraisal of the obsolescences which constitute the afterbirth of the new age. The survey must begin with man himself. "The proper study of Mankind is Man," said Pope. No amount of tinkering with his institutions will be sufficient to insure his survival unless he can make the necessary adjustments in his own relationship to the world and to society.

The first adjustment to be considered concerns man's savagely competitive impulses. Some may contend that this adjustment is impossible since it involves some of man's deepest instincts. Rousseau and Locke and Hobbes may be cited as authorities for the statement that man is basically individualist and competitive. It may be argued that it is futile to ask that man attempt to run counter to nature.

The anthropologists, however, will answer by denying that man is instinctively individualist. They contend that a study of man reveals his nature to be gregarious. His entire history, in fact, tells of one long, uninterrupted struggle to shatter his loneliness. It is only through his conditioning and environment that he has acquired his individualist habits. Even here, there is no reason inherent in nature why habits acquired cannot be replaced or redirected. We say "redirected" because not all his individualist or competitive habits are unhealthy or dangerous. When directed to creative and social ends, they can serve the purposes of progress, for competition can be an effective stimulus to constructive accomplishment. It is only when the competitive impulses or habits lose direction and become savagely anti-social that they constitute a destructive and ominous force.

So far as can be determined, those impulses are largely related to the rise of materialistic man, who has been a product —perhaps victim would be a better word—of his environment. Dominating this environment has always been an insufficiency of the goods and the needs of life. From Biblical days up through the present, there was never a time when starvation and economic suffering were not acute somewhere in the world, leading to conflict not only within nations but among nations.

This is only part of the story, of course, for it is dangerous to apply an economic interpretation indiscriminately to all history. Politics, religion, force for force's sake, jealousy, ambition, love of conquest, love of reform—all these and others have figured in the equations of history and war. But the economic factor was seldom if ever absent, even when it was not the prime mover. Populations frequently increased more rapidly than available land, goods, work, or wealth. Malthus believed that they increased so rapidly at times that war or plague or natural disaster became nature's safety valve.

YET ALL this has been—or can be—changed by the new age. Man now has it within his grasp to emancipate himself economically. If he wills it, he is in a position to redirect his competitive impulses; he can take the step from competitive man to co-operative man. He has at last unlocked enough of the earth's secrets to provide for his needs on a world scale. The same atomic and electrical energy that can destroy a continent can also usher in an age of economic sufficiency. It need no

The first and last of all life's complicated circumstances, the presiding fact, utterly astonishing, even stupefying, is that we are wholly in the dark about everything. Blank ignorance is our portion. In reasoning from the experience of nature and ourselves, we have all the evidence there is. We can add none. There remains, then, the reasoning itself, which is philosophy.

—W. MACNEILE DIXON, "The Human Situation" (1937)

longer be a question as to which peoples shall prosper and which shall be deprived. There are resources enough and power enough for all.

It is here that man's survey of himself needs the severest scrutiny, for he is his own greatest obstacle to the achievement of those attainable and necessary goals. While he is willing to mobilize all his scientific and intellectual energies for purposes of death, he has so far been unwilling to undertake any comparable mobilization for purposes of life. He has opened the atom and harnessed its fabulous power to a bomb, but he balks—or allows himself to be balked—when it comes to harnessing that power for human progress. Already, he has been given words of synthetic caution. Even as he stands on the threshold of a new age, he is pulled back by his coat-tails and told to look the other way, told that he will not see the practical application of atomic energy for general use in our lifetime. If it works out this way, it will not be because of any lack of knowledge or skill, but only because of the reluctance in certain quarters to face up to the full implications of the Atomic Age which does not exempt the economic structure any more than it exempts man himself.

The change now impending is in many ways more sweeping than that of the Industrial Revolution itself. And the irony is that man is asked to adjust himself to an Atomic Age before he has caught up with, let alone mastered, the age ushered in by electricity and steam.

Before 1830, change in man's way of life was almost imperceptible. A wheel turned no faster in Hannibal's time than it did in George Washington's. It took just as long to cultivate a wheat field in Egypt in 5000 B.C. as it did anywhere at the turn of the nineteenth century. The clothing worn by any of the Roman Caesars could not have been made more quickly until the invention of machines more than fifteen hundred years later. The speed of technological change was almost as slow as that of life itself.

Then suddenly, with the utilization of steam and electricity, more changes were made in technology in two generations than in all the thousands of years of previous human history put together. Wheels and machines turned so fast that man could cover more distances in one day than he used to be able to do in a lifetime. Fields that once defied many men were brought under cultivation through the use of machines. Some idea of the extent of these changes and the clipped brevity with which they took place may be gained by comparing them with previous technological milestones in human history. It took at least five hundred years to develop a knowledge of metallurgy; and approximately the same period for man to learn the science of chipping flints. But metallurgy and flint-chipping imposed no burden on the evolutionary intelligence of man, for they came too slowly to present any problem. As Alfred North Whitehead observes in his *Adventures of Ideas*, "The time span of important change was considerably longer than that of a single human life. Thus mankind was trained to adapt itself to fixed conditions. Today, this time-span is considerably shorter than that of human life, and accordingly, our training must prepare individuals to face a novelty of conditions."

And yet, says Whitehead, our social, economic, and political institutions are being developed on a time-span of change that was adequate in a pre-Industrial Revolution Age. We are suffering, he adds, from the "vicious assumption that each generation will substantially live amid the conditions governing the lives of its fathers and will transmit those conditions to mould with equal force the lives of its children. We are living in the first period of human history for which this assumption is false."

If all this was crucial even before the Atomic Age, consider how the problem has now been multiplied until its very dimensions almost seem beyond human comprehension. And if unchanging economic man was groping before in attempting to operate his society, consider the limitless wilderness in which he finds himself now. Little wonder that there has been so much of a disposition in some quarters to retreat from the atom, to pretend that it has little or no economic significance for the world of today.

However great our reluctance to acknowledge the birth of the new age, the fact is that it is already here. What remains to be decided is whether we are going to stand up to it and meet it head on, or whether we are going to back into it; whether we should fulfill its responsibilities and develop its promise, or whether we should try to circumvent it on the theory that what we don't think about can't hurt us; whether we should carry on atomic research for practical use with the same urgency, the same fullness, the same scope and intensity as we have for destructive use, or whether we should restrict atomic research to purposes of war.

If these questions are decided affirmatively, then the long over-due mobilization of science for man's needs—principally health—can and should be promptly started. For the size of the opportunity is exceeded only by the size of the need. What a bitter commentary—not on science but on society itself—that man has pierced the secret of atomic energy but is still baffled by the common cold! Who can tell what advances in medical knowledge might accrue to the welfare of mankind if society enabled its scientists and doctors to put as much mobilized effort into the study of man as there has been of matter! Cancer, heart disease, nephritis, arthritis, leukemia, encephalitis, poliomyelitis, arteriosclerosis, aplastic anemia—all these are anomalies in the modern world; there is no reason why mobilized research should not be directed at their causes and cure. Nor is there any reason why even old age should not be regarded as a disease to be attacked by science in the same intensive fashion.

Surveying other adjustments he will have to make if he chooses the positive course, man must consider himself in relation to his individual development. Leisure is a gift given him by technology; now he has the limitless opportunities that can come with time to think. The trend during the last fifty years toward shorter work weeks and shorter hours will not only be continued but sharply accelerated. No more than half of each week will be spent earning a living. But a revolution is needed in man's leisure-time activities—which so far have come to be associated almost entirely with the commodities of vended amusement. Once before, the world knew a Golden Age where the development of the individual—his mind and his body—was considered the first law of life. In Greece, it took the form of the revolution of awareness, the emancipation of the intellect from the limitations of corroding ignorance and prejudice.

Once again, if man wills it, he can be in a position to restore that first law of life. But he will have to effect a radical transformation in his approach to and philosophy of education, which should prepare him not only for the business of work but

To see creatures, wiser indeed than the monkey, and more active than the oyster, claiming to themselves the mastery of heaven; minims, the tenants of an atom, thus arrogating a partnership in the creation of universal Nature!

—Oliver Goldsmith, "The Citizen of the World" (1762)

for the business of living itself. The primary aim should be the development of a critical intelligence. The futile war now going on in education between specialization and general study must be stopped. There need no longer be any conflict between the two. The individual will need both—specialization for the requirements of research, general knowledge for the requirements of living. As for the problem of time in which to accomplish these dual objectives, formalized education until the twenty-fifth or thirtieth year is doubtless indicated; but it should not abruptly end there. Education, like the capacity of the mind itself, has no rigid boundaries. Unlimited exploration should be the first imperative of any educational program.

One of the liabilities of modern education is that it has contributed to a dangerous compartmentalization both of knowledge and of progress. Dangerous, because what is needed today is an understanding of the interconnections and interrelationships within the entire province of organized knowledge. This understanding can help avoid a tragically compartmentalized approach to the building of a new world. Already, man is being offered unilateral solutions in terms of economics alone or politics alone or ideology alone or science alone or religion alone. But it is not Economic Man or Political Man or Ideological Man or Scientific Man or Religious Man by himself who holds the solution. Only the Whole Man is equipped to find and act on whatever solution may exist.

And the Whole Man requires whole education. This does not mean that he must become a specialist in every branch of the sciences and the arts, nor does it mean that specialization must give way to superficial general study. What it does mean is that over and above specialized training there is a vast area to be cultivated in making a new science of integration—a science built on the interdependence of knowledge. It stands to reason that if we are living in an interdependent world, we must educate for interdependent living.

WE HAVE saved for last the most crucial aspect of this general survey relating to the first course: the transformation or adjustment from national man to world man. At present he is a world warrior; it is time for him to grow up and to become a world citizen. This is not vaporous idealism, but sheer driving necessity. It bears directly on the prospects of his own survival. He will have to recognize the flat truth that the greatest obsolescence of all in the Atomic Age is national sovereignty. Even back in the old-fashioned Rocket Age before August 6, 1945, strict national sovereignty was an anomalous hold-over from the tribal instinct in nations. If it was anomalous then, it is preposterous now.

It is preposterous because we have invested it with nonexistent powers. We assume that national sovereignty is still the same as it always was, that it still offers security and freedom of national decision. We assume it still means national independence, the right to get into war or stay out of it. We even debate the question of "surrendering" some of our sovereignty—as though there is still something to surrender. There is nothing left to surrender. There is only something to gain. A common world sovereignty.

At the heart of sovereignty throughout history there has been security based on the advantages of geography or military might. For sovereignty has been inseparable from power. But by the end of World War I, the validity of national sovereignty had sharply changed. The development of air power alone, apart from all other aspects of the world's inexorable trend toward close interrelationship, outdated traditional concepts of independence among nations. Yet we preferred to believe that there was no connection between a world being locked into a single piece and its over-all organization. Unfortunately, our unreadiness or unwillingness to see this connection did not cause the connection to disappear.

So much did this connection exist that it led to World War II. Despite six years of that new war, despite jet planes,

If, before the discovery of cannon, one had described its effects in the following manner: "There is a new invention, by which walls and the greatest bulwarks can be shaken and overthrown from a considerable distance," it is improbable that any imagination or fancy would have hit upon a fiery blast expanding and developing itself so suddenly and violently, because none would have seen an instance at all resembling it, except perhaps in earthquakes or thunder, which they would have immediately rejected as the great operations of nature, not to be imitated by man.

The human mind is often so awkward and ill regulated in the career of invention, that it is at first diffident, and then despises itself. For it appears at first incredible that it should so long have escaped man's research. All which affords good reason for the hope that a vast mass of inventions yet remains, which may be deduced not only from the investigation of new modes of operation, but also from transferring, comparing, and applying those already known, by the method of what we have termed literate experience.

Let men only consider: if they would apply only a small portion of the infinite expenditure of talent, time and fortune now given to matters and studies of far inferior importance and value, to sound and solid learning, it would be sufficient to overcome every difficulty.

—Francis Bacon, *Novum Organum* (1620)

rocket planes, despite the abrupt telescoping of a thousand years of human history in the release of atomic energy, despite the loss of millions of lives, still active as though sovereignty can function as it did two thousand years ago.

Can it be that we do not realize that in an age of atomic energy and rocket planes the foundations of the old sovereignties have been shattered? That no longer is security to be found in armies and navies, however large and mighty? That no longer is there security based on size and size alone? That any nation, however small, with atomic energy, is potentially as powerful as any other nation, however large? That in an Atomic Age all nations are now directly accessible to each other—for better or worse? That in the erasure of man-

◇◇

Lay then the axe to the root, and teach governments humanity.

The duty of man is not a wilderness of turnpike gates through which he is to pass by tickets from one to the other. It is plain and simple, and consists of but two points. His duty to God, which every man must feel; and with respect to his neighbor, to do as he would be done by.

That which is called government, or rather that which we ought to conceive government to be, is no more than some common center in which all the parts of society unite . . . It concentrates the knowledge necessary to the interests of the parts and of the whole. It places government in a state of constant maturity. It is never young, never old. It is subject neither to nonage nor dotage. It is never in the cradle nor on crutches. It admits not of a separation between knowledge and power, and is superior, as government ought always to be, to all the accidents of individual man.

—Thomas Paine, "The Rights of Man" (1791)

◇◇

made barriers and boundaries all the peoples of the world stand virtually unarmed in the presence of one another? That they are at the mercy of one another, and shall have to devise a common security or suffer a common cataclysm? That the only really effective influence between peoples is such influence as they are able to exert morally, politically, ideologically upon each other? That the use of disproportionate wealth and abundance of resources by any nation, when applied for bargaining purposes, do not constitute influence but the type of coercion against which severe reaction is inevitable?

All these questions have been in the making for centuries, but the triumph over the invisible and mighty atom has given them an exactness and an immediacy about which there can be no mistake. The need for world government was clear long before August 6, 1945, but Hiroshima and Nagasaki raised that need to such dimensions that it can no longer be ignored. And in the glare brighter than sunlight produced by the assault on the atom, we have all the light we need with which to examine this new world that has come into being with such clicking abruptness. Thus examined, the old sovereignties are seen for what they are—vestigial obstructions in the circulatory system of the world.

MUCH of the attachment to old concepts of sovereignty, as well as the reluctance to face squarely its severe limitations in the modern world, grows out of apprehension over the control a world authority might have over the internal affairs of the individual state. There is the fear, for example, that the individual Constitutions would be subject to central control. There is the fear that institutions built up over centuries would exist only at the pleasure and discretion of a super-state.

Natural and understandable though these concerns may be, they have their source in confusion over a distinction that should be made between world *sovereignty* and state *jurisdiction.* A common world sovereignty would mean that no state could act unilaterally in its foreign affairs. It would mean that no state could have the instruments of power to aggress against other states. It would mean that no state could withdraw from the central authority as a method of achieving its aims. But it would *not* mean that the individual state would lose its *jurisdiction* over its internal affairs. It would *not* mean the arbitrary establishment of a uniform ideology all over the world. It would *not* mean the forcible imposition of non-democratic systems on democratic states, any more than it would mean the forcible imposition of democratic systems on non-democratic states.

Though the idea of bestowing democracy on all other peoples throughout the world seems both magnanimous and attractive, the fact remains that democracy is not to be had just for the giving or the taking. It cannot be donated or imposed from without. It is an intricate and highly advanced mechanism capable of existing, like man himself, under certain conditions. It depends not only on the love of freedom, but on the ability to carry the responsibilities of freedom. It requires enduring respect for numberless principles, not all of them incorporated into formal law. It requires adherence to the principle of majority rule with preservation of minority rights. It is as much a way of living and a philosophy of life as it is a form of political organization.

This does not mean, however, that peoples not now democratic must be restrained from moving toward democracy. Nor does it mean that the conditions under which democracy can come into being cannot be nurtured and developed. So far as a central authority is concerned, one way to help in that development can be by providing a greater external harmony that will permit a greater internal harmony.

In creating this higher sovereignty, we naturally wonder whether history has any advice to offer. History tells of two experiences worth our examination. The first happened in Greece more than two thousand years ago; the second happened in America a century and a half ago. Neither experience can properly be termed a parallel or a precise guide to the present. Strictly speaking, no precise guide to the present is to be found anywhere. Never before has the world known such profound and sudden shocks; never before has there been so little in the way of previous experience to build upon. But while we should not overstretch historical analogy, neither should we fail to take into account the operation of certain historical principles whose validity might seem to apply to our own time.

Early Greece—that is, the Greece of the pre-Christian era—was not a state but a bundle of states. Though geographically united, it was politically disunited, with trade rivalries and frequent wars. The need for one nation to rise out of all the small city-states was apparent to many Greek leaders, but no one city-state was willing to take the initiative in building a genuine, common sovereignty. Several leagues or confederations were attempted, but broke down because the strongest states arrogated supreme power to themselves. Moreover, leagues of nations were arrayed against each other within Greece itself, with small states in the south clustered around Sparta, and the small states in the north clustered around Athens. This struggle between Athens and Sparta, growing

◇◇

Truth never yet fell dead in the streets; it has such affinity with the soul of man, the seed however broadcast will catch somewhere and produce its hundred-fold.

—Theodore Parker (1810–1816)

◇◇

out of their inability to come together within a single governmental organization, cost Greek civilization its very life.

Greece's failure is worth noting because it illustrates the consequences of disunion for states within a related group. It is worth noting, too, because it served as one of the strongest arguments for a union of the states during the making of the American Constitution. Throughout the minutes of the Constitutional Convention, and throughout *The Federalist*, which interpreted and analyzed the work of the convention, we find frequent reference to the Greek experience.

The causes and the effects of the Greek failure, said *The Federalist*, "cannot be too highly colored, or too often exhibited. Every man who loves peace, every man who loves his country, every man who loves liberty, ought to have it ever before his eyes . . ." Readers were told that if the Greeks had been "as wise as they were courageous," they would have transformed their loose and competing leagues into a real union. *The Federalist* believed that had such a union been formed after the war against Persia, when both Athens and Sparta were, for once, united in defense of Greece, there might never have been a Peloponnesian War culminating in the ruin of both states and in the decay of Greece itself. America, said *The Federalist*, should be the "broad and solid foundation of other edifices, not less magnificent, which will be equally permanent monuments of their errors."

The mutual dependence of man is so great in all societies that scarce any human action is entirely complete in itself, or is performed without some reference to the actions of others.

—David Hume, "An Enquiry Concerning Human Understanding" (1748)

There is a disposition to deny the value of America's success at international organization one hundred and sixty years ago because the states were supposedly so compact, so homogeneous, so closely knit in their cultural and political and economic patterns.

Let us see.

There were thirteen American nations in the Revolution against England. They came out of that Revolution as former allies rather than as partners in a continuing enterprise. There were varying and frequently conflicting systems of political, economic, monetary, and social organization. Sovereignty, separation, sectarianism—these fixed the thinking of the day. A man who went from one state to another found that his currency would shrink ten per cent just in the act of crossing a state line. At one point, Vermont, New Hampshire, and New York were on the brink of war. In the absence of an outside threat after the Revolution, the colonies began to fall apart.

Frederick Scott Oliver, in his study of Alexander Hamilton as a federationist, tells us that, "the citizens hardened their hearts, preferring, like Pharaoh, to endure the murrain, the locusts, and the darkness, rather than abandon their mean jealousies, their rivalries at once sordid and malicious; rather than part with a single shred of local sovereignty to clothe the shivering and naked form of federal government. . . . Finally, in their madness, they fell upon each other; each at the beginning looking merely for advantage to itself in injury to its neighbors, even as an end in itself."

In all the discussion over the making of America, a fact frequently overlooked is that the American Revolution did not create the United States. The United States were created largely through their differences, differences so intense that only a common sovereignty could prevent international anarchy within the American group.

John Fiske, in his *Critical Period of American History,* writes that each little city or district regarded itself as an island. "Local prejudices were intense. It was not simply free Massachusetts and slave-holding South Carolina, or English Connecticut and Dutch New York, that misunderstood and ridiculed each other, but even between such neighboring states as Connecticut and Massachusetts, both of them thoroughly English and Puritan, and in all their social conditions almost exactly alike, it used often to be said that there was no love lost. These unspeakably stupid and contemptible local antipathies are inherited by civilized men from that far-off time when the clan system prevailed over the face of the earth and the hand of every clan was raised against its neighbor. They are pale and evanescent survivals from the universal primitive warfare, and the sooner they die out from human society, the better for every one."

Or listen to Thomas Paine on the "homogeneous" quality of

The ultimate aim of government is not to rule, nor to restrain by fear, nor to exact obedience, but contrariwise, to free every man from fear, that he may live in all possible security; in other words, to strengthen his natural right to exist and to work without injury to himself or others. No, the object of government is not to change men from rational beings into beasts or puppets, but to enable them to develop their minds and bodies in security, and to employ their reason unshackled; neither showing hatred, anger, or deceit, nor watched with the eyes of jealousy and injustice. In fact, the true aim of government is liberty.

—Baruch Spinoza, "Writings on Political Philosophy" (1670)

---

the Colonial peoples at the time the international organization that is the United States was founded:

"If there is a country in the world where concord, according to common calculation, would be least expected, it is America. Made up, as it is, of people from different nations, accustomed to different forms and habits of government, speaking different languages, and more different in their modes of worship, it would appear that the union of such a people was impracticable. But by the simple operation of constructing government on the principles of society and the rights of man, every difficulty retires, and the parts are brought into cordial unison."

Paine's footnote to this paragraph indicates that the melting pot was not peculiar to a later period in American history. "That part of America," he said, "which is generally called New England, including New Hampshire, Massachusetts, Rhode Island, and Connecticut, is peopled chiefly by English descendants. In the state of New York, about half are Dutch, the rest English, Scotch and Irish. In New Jersey, a mixture of English and Dutch, with some Scotch and Irish. In Pennsylvania, about one-third are English, another third German, and the remainder Scotch and Irish, with some Swedes. The states to the southward have a greater proportion of English than the middle states, but in all of them there is a mixture; and besides those enumerated, there are a considerable number of French, and some few of all the European nations, lying on the Coast."

Paine went on to point out that the American experience proved that diverse peoples did not have to be subjugated to be brought together, but that they could achieve common government through common consent. Government, he said, was not a "thing made up of mysteries," but a "national association acting on the principles of society."

In examining, therefore, the Greek and American experiences, we find one central point worth considering in relation to the problem before us today: States within a related group must live as one or suffer as many. A corollary is that the differences among peoples are not a deterrent in meeting the need for over-all government, but actually both a pre-condition and a basic reason behind the need.

What validity does this have for the world today? First, do the nations of the world belong to a related group? If so, how and to what extent?

The world has at last become a geographic unit, if we measure geographic units not according to absolute size but according to access and proximity. All peoples are members of this related group, just as the thirteen American colonies belonged to a related group, and just as the city-states of Greece belonged to a related group. The extent of this relationship need only be measured by the direct access nations have to each other for purposes of war. And the consequences of disunion are as applicable to the world group today as they were to individual groupings of states in the past. The unorganized geographic units of the past have given way to the unorganized unit of the present. It is a unit without unity, an order without any order.

In a world where it takes less time to get from New York to Chungking than it took to get from New York to Philadelphia in 1787, the nature and extent of this geographic entity becomes apparent. All natural distances and barriers vanish. Never before in history has the phrase, the human family, had such a precise meaning. This much all of us—American, European, African, Asiatic, Australian—have in common: Whether we like it or not, we have been brought together or thrust together as members of a world unit, albeit an unorganized world unit. Within that unit, to be sure, are divisions and subdivisions, but they are all heavily interdependent. There is little point in musing or speculating whether this unit is desirable or whether it deserves our support. The fact is that it exists.

Here we must meet the argument that even though the world may be a geographical unit, it is too large, too unwieldy, for the creation and operation of a governmental unit. But size alone does not limit the area in which government can function. Unwieldiness is entirely relative to the instruments of control. For harmony among states depends upon relationships; and relationships among states depend upon law and respect for law.

No less an authority on international organization than *The Federalist* tells us that "the larger the society, provided it be within a practical sphere, the more duly capable will it be of self-government." By "practical," *The Federalist* meant both necessity and workability. Thus a state could be as large as

◇◇

What constitutes a State?
Not high-raised battlement, or labored mound,
Thick wall or moated gate;
Nor cities fair, with spires and turrets crown'd;
No:—Men, high-minded men,
With powers as far above dull brutes endued
In forest, brake or den,
As beasts excel cold rocks and brambles rude:—
Men who their duties know,
But know their rights, and knowing, dare maintain;
Prevent the long-aimed blow,
And crush the tyrant, while they rend the chain.

—ALCAEUS, "The State," (c. 600 B.C.)
as adapted by Sir William Jones

◇◇

the need behind it, so long as it possesses effective machinery for its administration. And two thousand years before *The Federalist,* Aristotle considered the limitations upon the size of a state and decided that it could be determined by the range of a man's voice. Accessibility seemed to Aristotle to be the prime requisite of a governmental unit. According to this definition, radio has converted the entire world into a small enclosure capable of central government. But radio is only one of the instruments available for drawing the peoples of the world together under a common sovereignty. The revolution in transportation can give them a mutuality such as even the people of any one nation a hundred or more years ago never knew among themselves.

This mutuality—a mutuality built on present and future needs—is more important than physical dimensions. A common ground of destiny is not too large a site for the founding of any community.

But reject all other arguments for world government—reject the geographic, economic, the ideological, the sociological, the humanitarian arguments, valid though they may be. Consider only the towering job of policing the atom—the job of keeping the smallest particle of matter from destroying all matter. This means control. But control is no natural phenomenon. It does not operate of and by itself. Control is impossible without power—the power of investigation, the power

---

I know no safe depository of the ultimate powers of society but the people themselves; and if we think them not enlightened enough to exercise their control with a wholesome direction, the remedy is not to take it from them, but to inform their discretion by education.

—Thomas Jefferson, Letter (1820)

---

of injunction, the power of arrest, the power of punishment.

But power, like control, cannot be isolated, nor is it desirable except under carefully defined circumstances. Power must be subordinate to law, unless it is to take the form of brute, irresponsible force. Here, too, we are involved in an important interrelationship, because law can be derived only through government. Law is a product of moral, judicial, executive, legislative, and administrative sanction—all of which adds up to government. And government means what it says: the process of governing. It is not decentralization, it is not informal organization, it is not the right of veto or the right of secession by any state or states. It is a central body none of whose members has the right or the means of aggression or withdrawal. It is the source of legitimate action and legitimate redress.

Approach the problem in reverse. We are all agreed that war must be "outlawed." If that is what we really mean, then we shall have to apply law. Law based on what? On general agreement? With or without sanctions? With or without protective as well as punitive power? With or without a judiciary? To the extent that the answers to these questions are subtractive, we shall fail in our agreed purpose. Outlawry of war is a noble phrase but its translation into tangible effectiveness requires, by its very nature, the existence of the basis and the instruments of legality, by which we mean government.

We are left, then, with three basic principles necessarily related to an effective system of international control:

No control without power.
No power without law.
No law without government.

ARE there no other practicable methods of control? Is atomic power such a menace that nothing less than world government may be able to deal with it? What less drastic plans have been suggested?

Before examining these questions, bear in mind that the atom bomb dropped on Nagasaki represented a substantial improvement over the Hiroshima model. Bear in mind that the first atomic bomb, admittedly still in the experimental stage and said to weigh only a few pounds, was the equivalent of 20,000 tons of the most effective TNT explosive ever previously developed. Bear in mind that more than eighty per cent of the world's supply of uranium is located outside the United States, Canada, and Great Britain, which share the distinction and the responsibility for unleashing atomic energy. Bear in mind that other nations, Japan included, have already experimented successfully with plutonium, a derivative of uranium.

Bear in mind that United States territory is no longer safe from bombing attack. Bear in mind that more than four hundred Japanese balloons carrying not atomic but incendiary bombs were able to perform their explosive missions over the western portion of the United States, some being carried as far east as Michigan—although only a small number caused effective damage. Bear in mind that Japan was getting ready to launch long-range, one-way, heavy bombers for a direct attack on the United States when the atomic bombs ended the war. Bear in mind that it is possible *today* to develop pilotless rocket planes, carrying huge explosive atomic cargoes; and that these planes, from their launching stations, will be capable of hitting any specified target area in the world within the radius of a single mile.

Bear in mind that it would require only an infinitesimal percentage of the number of bombing missions in World War II for rocket planes to lay waste every city in the world—not in a matter of months or weeks or even days, but hours. Bear in mind that most military experts predict that within three years —five years at the most—knowledge of utilization of atomic energy may be as commonplace as present-day knowledge of aviation itself.

Bear all this in mind and then consider what would be required to safeguard the world from destructive atomic energy. Consider various suggestions advanced as possible methods of control. Begin by considering the fairly popular theory that every weapon produces a counter-weapon, and that in the course of time the atomic bomb will meet its match in some sort of super-atomic defense. This is by far the coziest, most convenient, approach to the problem. It requires almost no physical and mental exertion and doubtless has its origin in

◇◇

A dispute once arose between the Wind and the Sun, as to which was the stronger of the two, and they agreed to put the point upon this issue, that whichever soonest made a traveller take off his cloak should be judged the more powerful. The Wind began, and blew with all his might and main a blast, cold and fierce as a Thracian storm; but the stronger he blew the closer the traveller wrapped his cloak around him, and the tighter he grasped it with his hands. Then broke out the Sun. With his welcome beams he dispersed the vapor and the cold; the traveller felt the genial warmth and as the Sun shone brighter and brighter, he sat down, flushed with the heat, and cast his cloak upon the ground.

Thus the Sun was declared the conqueror; and it has ever been deemed that persuasion is better than mere force; and that the sunshine of a warm and helpful manner will sooner lay open a poor man's heart than all the threatenings and force of blustering authority.

—Aesop's Fables (c. 580 b.c.)

◇◇

the pleasant belief that everything will come out all right in the end—atomic bombs and rocket planes not excluded. Absurd as the theory seems, it nevertheless requires a sober and serious answer; every shred of hope must be fully and carefully appraised at a time when all hope sorely needs definition and direction.

The obvious answer to the counter-weapon argument is that we can take nothing for granted. We cannot assume the automatic development of such a device, and among those who are the least sanguine in this respect are the scientists themselves. Nor is it true that every new weapon in history has been equated by another weapon. Air power was far ahead of anti-aircraft not only after World War I but after World War II. The only effective answer to air power was more air power, but this did not prevent cities from being leveled during the struggle for air supremacy. Nor did it prevent robots and rocket bombs from taking lives until the invasion of the European Continent overran the launching stations. But the cardinal fallacy of the counter-weapon theory is that it assumes there may be enough time in which to bring the negating devices into play—even granting the possibility of their development.

Modern warfare's only effective counter-weapon is retaliation, and there may not even be time for that, once an attack begins, for the beginning may be the ending as well.

It is said that man can go underground in an atomic war, that he can carve out large cities under the surface of the earth and at the first sign of danger can retire to subterranean shelters and stay there indefinitely if need be. Ingenious cut-away and cross-section sketches have been published, revealing vast improvements over the crude World War II underground shelters. The new shelters will have all conveniences, including hot and cold running water, refrigeration, and moving-picture theaters. But the sketches failed to explain how it would be possible to burrow far enough into the earth to avoid the shattering concussive power of atomic violence. They failed to tell what would happen to those underground cities once the exploded atom left an inextinguishable fire on the crust of the earth. If any imaginative sketches are in order at all, let us see some which can speculate upon the amount of fire and bombarding and atom-splitting a weary planet can absorb without being thrown off its axis or without reverting to its original incandescent mass blazing at millions of degrees.

It is claimed that warfare has now become so horrible that no nation will dare to unleash it. The argument is not new; it was heard when the bow and arrow were used in Egypt more than five thousand years ago. It was heard when the phalanx was developed to supposedly invincible strength in Macedonia more than two thousand years ago. It was heard when gunpowder was introduced more than five hundred years ago. It was heard less than thirty years ago after a World War in which dynamite took to the sky. But each time, though the horror of war increased, though the size of the battlefield grew larger and larger until the world itself became the arena of combat, new wars continued to break out.

So fallacious is the war-is-now-too-horrible theory that ac-

◇◇

Mankind as a whole has always striven to organize a universal state. There have been many great nations with great histories, but the more highly they were developed the more unhappy they were, for they felt more acutely than other people the craving for world-wide union.

—Fëdor Dostoevski, "The Grand Inquisitor" (1881)

◇◇

tually the reverse is true. The possibility of war increases in direct proportion to the effectiveness of the instruments of war. Far from banishing war, the atomic bomb may in itself constitute a cause of war. In the absence of world control, it may create universal fear and suspicion. Each nation may live nervously from one moment to the next, not knowing whether the designs or ambitions of other nations might prompt them to attempt a lightning blow of obliteration. The ordinary, the inevitable differences among nations which might in themselves be susceptible of solution might now become the signals for direct action, lest other nations get in the first and decisive blow. Since the science of warfare will no longer be dependent upon armies but will be waged by pushbuttons, releasing armadas of radio-controlled rocket planes carrying atomic explosives, the slightest suspicion may start all the pushbuttons going.

It will be argued that each nation will realize this; that is, that the first button might lead to universal catastrophe as all the other nations rush to the switchboards of annihilation. This presupposes the existence of reason—but reason is hardly something likely to flourish in a world of international anarchy, by which we mean the absence of central government. Moreover, there may always be the feeling that one nation can escape though all the others may go down. What a temptation for the blitzkriegers!

MORE popular than any of these suggestions for controlling the atom is the plea, advanced in Parliament and in Congress, that England and America keep the secret of the atomic bomb to themselves. Conspicuously absent among those urging such action are the scientists—not because they do not believe it may be desirable to retain exclusive possession of the bomb, but because they do not believe it is in our power to do so.

They know of Germany's advanced experiments with atomic energy; they know of Japan's development of plutonium; they know that the very demonstration of the successful fission of the atom is crucially valuable knowledge for other nations in rounding out their experiments; they know that in the very act of attempting to keep the mechanism of the atomic bomb a secret we stimulate other nations to undertake whatever additional research is necessary over their present experimentation to yield the desired results. They know, too, that in all history there is not a single instance of a new weapon being kept exclusively by any power or powers; sooner or later either the basic principles become generally known or parallel devices are invented. Before long, the atomic bomb will follow the jet plane, the rocket bomb, radar, and the flame thrower into general circulation. We were not the only horse in the atomic derby. We just happened to finish first; the others will be along in due time.

STILL another suggestion is that the nations of the world agree to a system of voluntary inspection. Behind this is the knowledge that it is difficult and almost impossible to hide the large laboratory and production facilities required to produce atomic bombs. It would be possible, according to this suggestion, to train a force of "atomic detectives" who would have freedom of examination anywhere in the world.

Even granting the infallibility of the inspectors to ferret out atomic bomb plants wherever they may be in the world, two weaknesses clamor for attention. The first is that any system of investigation is only as strong as the agency behind it. The agency in this case is nothing but a gentleman's agreement lacking executive and police power. The second weakness is that any nation at any time can revoke its part in the agreement and refuse admission to the inspection force.

So far, it will be observed that all the methods proposed have one thing in common. They all rest on naked chance. The chance that a counter-weapon may be developed. The chance that war will be self-liquidating because it has become so horrible. The chance that no other nation is smart enough to develop its own atomic weapons without our help. The chance that an inspection system can work with nothing behind it. At a time of dimensionless peril, we are asked to build on random chance.

In looking beyond random chance for a firmer footing on which to build for tomorrow, we naturally turn to the United Nations Charter. There can be little question that when the delegates from forty-four nations concluded their Conference at San Francisco in June 1945, they had made a promising start in the direction of international security. Whatever its imperfections, the Charter was a signal contribution to world peace. In the statement of its principles and objectives, in the provision of machinery for making it stronger and more effective, in the very fact that men from many lands had come together, reflecting the desire of peoples of every continent to plan for world peace as they had planned for victory in the war—in all these respects, the Charter was of historic importance. Moreover, so far as the United States was concerned, it kept the door of isolation from slamming abruptly in the faces of the American people.

It is no reflection on the Charter, or on the men who joined in its making, to say that it has become a feeble and antiquated instrument for dealing with the problems of an Atomic Age. It is no reflection, because even the calendar is hopelessly out of date. A thousand years of the world's history were compressed in that brief fraction of a second during which Hiroshima was leveled. The world which the San Francisco Conference met to consider no longer exists, even though the same nations and same people represented at the Conference belong to both the old and new worlds.

After the Charter was drafted, even its warmest advocates did not claim that it was equipped to cope with war or the threat of war. But it was felt that time might work to the advantage of the United Nations—time in which to build up the habit of peace, time in which to strengthen and implement the Charter so that within fifteen or twenty years it might take the form of a real and durable world structure.

But the time factor has been reversed. Time no longer works for peace. Time today works against peace. The longer we wait the more difficult it becomes to achieve world government. There is a desperate though quiet scramble in almost every nation of the world to duplicate the success of America, Canada, and Great Britain in prying open the atom. This race is not only based on distrust but generates distrust. The feeling grows everywhere that it must be every nation for itself. Are these the foundations of a common security? Are these the building blocks of lasting peace?

Do we realize that time is running out? Do we realize that victory has given us no real "respite," as has been claimed, but has created instead an emergency not less intense than the world knew at Dunkirk or Stalingrad or Pearl Harbor? Do we realize that victory imposed obligations from which we cannot shrink? These obligations are directly related to the responsibility we have to assume for the invention and use of the most hideously successful and indiscriminate killer in history. This is not so much a matter of justifying our use of the atomic bomb as it is a matter of following up the unprecedented use of raw power with real moral leadership. In short, it is the obligation and opportunity to equate the atomic bomb with an atomic solvent, to equate force with reason, stating to the peoples of the world the full implications as we understand them of atomic energy, and filling the vacuum created by the atomic bomb by calling upon them to join in the building of a real world structure for the greater welfare and safety of all.

THIS atomic solvent operates not through a chemical compound or a gadget but through an active world public opinion in bringing peoples together. Once the nature and imminency of the peril are clearly understood by the peoples of the world, their differences will not be a bar but an incentive to common government, as was demonstrated earlier in the case of the American colonies. For it is not in spite of these differences but because of them that the world is now in need of a general amalgam. The very purpose of government is to regulate differences. If these differences did not exist, if man's actions were uniform and uniformly predictable, then man would be as free of war as the vegetable kingdom. The differences point up the problem, not the problem the differences. The primary consideration is not how great an obstacle the differences may be to the setting up of a closely knit world structure, but whether men will be in a better position to reconcile those differences within world government than without it.

Moreover, there are few differences that confront nations in their dealings with each other that they do not have to meet within themselves. Man himself is a magnificent summing-up of differences, of which the larger differences on the international scale are only a reflection. Macneile Dixon, in *The Human Situation,* reminds us that "many are the races and many the temperaments. There are vehement and hot-headed men, selfless and conciliatory men. They display, varying as they do in appearance, talents, behavior, every type of unpredictable reaction to their surroundings. There are sybarites and ascetics, dreamers and bustling men of affairs, clever and stupid, worldly and religious, mockers and mystics, pugnacious, loyal, cunning, treacherous, cheerful and melancholy men. There are eagles among them, tigers, doves, and serpents. 'He was a comedian on the stage,' said the wife of a celebrated funny man, 'but a tragedian in the home.' "

World government will not and cannot dissolve these differences. All it can do is operate on a level which can keep those differences, when raised to international dimensions, from dissolving the globe itself.

This is the propitious moment, the grand moment, with the tremendous psychological advantages it offers at the end of a great war, to take the moral leadership in bringing the atomic solvent into play. But that propitious moment is slipping. The world is slipping, too—back into old systems of power politics and spheres of influence—the ovaries of war.

By itself and of itself, the United Nations Charter cannot arrest this trend. Nor would any amount of implementation do the job so long as nations can act unilaterally and so long as nations can withdraw from the over-all organization at their own discretion. Nor can we sit back comfortably and wait several generations for the world to evolve naturally and progressively into a single governmental unit which would erase those dangerous privileges. Whatever is done must be done with an immediacy which is in keeping with the urgency. Not another Conference but a Constitutional Convention of the

◇◇◇

To kill one's fellow creatures needs no great genius; but to calm a tempest by prudence and judgment is a worthy achievement indeed.

—ERASMUS, Letters (c. 1500)

◇◇◇

United Nations is needed—not only to undertake a general inventory of the revolutionary changes in the world since the San Francisco meeting in the long-ago spring of 1945, but to design the form and fabric of real government.

The difficulties confronting such a Convention would be far and away the most comprehensive and complicated that any group of men anywhere, at any time, have had to face. But of one thing the Convention can be certain, and that is a knowledge of what failure will mean. The Convention has some advantage, too, in knowing that if world government sounds as though it poses methods or solutions above the reach of mortal man, some answer is to be found in the fact that the reach of mortal man was long enough apparently to push science and invention ahead by perhaps a thousand years during a few years of experimentation with atomic energy. His ability to do this not only indicates that he can extend or overextend himself when pressed, but emphasizes the need to do the same with government.

There is no need to discuss the historical reasons pointing to and arguing for world government. There is no need to talk of the difficulties in the way of world government. There is need only to ask whether we can afford to do without it. All other considerations become either secondary or inconsequential.

There comes to mind a scene from one of the old "silent" films. An outcast, lost somewhere in a mountainous forest, stands on the edge of a canyon. Behind him rages a forest fire, drawing ever closer. In front of him is a sheer drop of several hundred feet. But the gap across this canyon to the other side is only ten feet wide. Ten feet! He has never jumped ten feet before. He has no way of knowing that he can jump it now. He has no choice but to try.

The precise outcome of this episode we are unable to tell, for it was one of those Saturday afternoon adventure serials which was discontinued at just the crucial second. But we never entertained any doubts that at least the jump was attempted.

MANKIND today is involved in a somewhat similar predicament. It would be comforting to believe that we could leisurely build a footbridge across the gap. It would be comforting to believe that time is working in our favor, or that the fire has changed its direction. But it happens that there is no time to build a footbridge. It happens that we cannot take just a step forward but must jump. It happens that the longer we delay the less space we shall have for a running leap. It happens that if we wait too long we shall have the disadvantage of jumping from a stationary position. Perhaps we have never jumped ten feet before. But under the circumstances that is the poorest of all reasons not to try.

And even if we make the jump successfully, we still have not disposed of all our problems. For though world government provides a better method and a better chance of preserving world peace than man has ever possessed, it cannot provide a guarantee of world peace. It provides man with time—time to think, time to change, time to keep decisions in his own hands, but it cannot make the right decisions for him. It provides only the minimum and not the maximum requirements of a common security. It provides the broad and solid ground in which to sink the foundations of a genuine sovereignty, and on which to build a floor under tomorrow; but it does not provide a finished structure. It provides the form but not the substance. That finished structure and that substance can be provided only by the vision and the day-by-day wisdom of man himself.

Peace under world government is only half the job. Peace is a big word; there are all kinds of peace. Peace can be slavery or it can be freedom; subjugation or liberation. It can be static or dynamic, stagnant or vibrant. Alfred North Whitehead once described peace without purpose as "anesthesia." The real peace is more than non-war. It is a vital peace, a restlessness to get on with the work of the world, an anxiety to meet the future. The real peace means progress. That is the other half of the job.

Directly related to the danger of a purposeless peace is the danger represented by a perverted use of power. World government requires the manipulation of power on a larger scale than man has ever known, but unless this power is carefully defined, unless it is surrounded with workable checks and balances, unless it is *representative* rather than *dictatorial,* unless it is subject to changes in its officers and in its laws in response to changing needs and the freely expressed will of the peoples of the states—it can lead to a world tyranny against which insurrection will be difficult if not impossible. The instruments of control will have been necessarily concentrated and centralized in order to guard against the use of unlimited destructive power in the hands of lawless forces, but those same weapons can become the instruments by which a tyranny might attempt to entrench itself and enforce its decisions.

The prospect is frightening, but it is a problem man has had to face in the creation or operation of government on any level. Power inevitably constitutes an invitation to tyranny, whether on a community or a national or an international scale. The crucial question is whether the need for power exists, and, if so, what type of power will be used, how, and by whom? In starting World War II, Germany recognized that the world had become a geographic unit; and it was her intention to organize and rule the world order. The power in that case would have been exercised even more arbitrarily outside Germany than it had been inside Germany. But in defeating the Axis, we did not automatically destroy the need for power on a world scale any more than we destroyed the geographic world unit itself. We succeeded only in creating the opportunity to refine and channel that power through properly constituted and representative government. If we refuse to meet or fail to meet this opportunity, we automatically create a vacuum which will be filled by a single nation or bloc of nations, or which will result in crude international anarchy.

All through history there has been too great a contradiction between ideals and the forces which have taken over those ideals. Another way of saying this is that too often we have allowed the best ideals to fall into the hands of the worst men. There has scarcely been a great ideal or idea which has not been perverted or exploited at one time or another by those who were looking for means to an end. The greatest idea ever to be taken up by the mind of man—Christianity—was for centuries violated and corrupted by its very administrators. Alexander's vision of a brotherhood of man fell victim to its own force—force based on might makes right. Mohammed dreamed of a religion based on the noblest of ethics, yet his followers built an empire largely at the point of the sword. Surveying the immediate past, we observe that it was in the name of socialism and social progress that Fascism came to Italy and Nazism to Germany.

So that we return full circle to man himself, to the animal that must operate the world government. Is he wise enough to use greater power for greater good? Is he wise enough to create a common sovereignty and yet keep the ultimate power in his own hands?

This is the multiple nature of the challenge to modern man—to bring about world government and to keep it pure; to keep his social, economic, and political institutions apace with his scientific achievements; to make whatever adjustments are needed in his own make-up, conditioning, and outlook on life in order to exist in an Atomic Age.

This is a large order, perhaps the largest order man has had to fill in his fifty thousand-odd years on earth, but he himself has set up the conditions which have made the order necessary. We can put on blinders; we can laugh it all off as just a false alarm; we can claim that talk of an Atomic Age is sheer fancy; we can protest that the threat of the destructive use of atomic energy is exaggeration, overstatement, hysteria, panic.

But all the manufactured calm and scorn in the world cannot alter the precise fact that the atomic bomb plus another war equals global disaster. Nor that the crisis is fast approaching and may be upon us within a few years unless we act now to avert it. Nor that this crisis is created not only by the explosive atom but by inadequate means of controlling international lawlessness. Nor that control is inoperative without power, that power is dangerous without law, and that law is impossible without government.

Where the mind is without fear and the head is held high;
Where knowledge is free;
Where the world has not been broken up into fragments
by narrow domestic walls;
Where words come out from the depth of truth;
Where tireless striving stretches its arms toward perfection;
Where the clear stream of reason has not lost its way
into the dreary desert sand of dead habit;
Where the mind is led forward by thee into ever-widening
thought and action—
Into that heaven of freedom, my Father, let my country awake.

—RABINDRANATH TAGORE, "Gitanjali" (1912)

AND if we reject the multiple challenge before us? And if we decide that we are not yet ready for world government? What then? Then there is yet another way, an alternative to world government, an alternative to change in man. This way is the second course. Absurd as this second course may seem, we describe it in all seriousness, for it is possible that through it man may find a way to stay alive—which is the central problem before us.

This second course is fairly simple. It requires that man eliminate the source of the trouble. Let him dissociate himself, carefully and completely, from civilization and all its works. Let him systematically abolish science and the tools of science. Let him destroy all machines and the knowledge which can build or operate those machines. Let him raze his cities, smash his laboratories, dismantle his factories, tear down his universities and schools, burn his libraries, rip apart his art. Let him murder his scientists, his lawmakers, his statesmen, his doctors, his teachers, his mechanics, his merchants, and anyone who has anything to do with the machinery of knowledge or progress. Let him punish literacy by death. Let him eradicate nations and set up the tribe as sovereign. Let him, in short, revert to his condition in society in 10,000 B.C. Thus emancipated from science, from progress, from government, from knowledge, from thought, he can be reasonably certain of prolonging his existence on this planet.

This can be a way out—if "modern" man is looking for a way out from the modern world.

APPENDIX

◇

Excerpts from

THE FEDERALIST

on

The Making of the Constitution

of the

UNITED STATES OF AMERICA

(1788)

◇◇◇

THE FEDERALIST

No. 14.—BY JAMES MADISON

An objection drawn from the extent of country answered.

WE HAVE seen the necessity of the Union, as our bulwark against foreign danger; as the conservator of peace among ourselves; as the guardian of our commerce, and other common interests; as the only substitute for those military establishments which have subverted the liberties of the old world; and as the proper antidote for the diseases of faction, which have proved fatal to other popular Governments, and of which alarming symptoms have been betrayed by our own.

All that remains, within this branch of our inquiries, is to take notice of an objection that may be drawn from the great extent of country which the Union embraces. A few observations on this subject, will be the more proper, as it is perceived, that the adversaries of the new Constitution are availing themselves of a prevailing prejudice, with regard to the practicable sphere of republican administration, in order to supply, by imaginary difficulties, the want of those solid objections, which they endeavour in vain to find. . . .

AS THE natural limit of a democracy, is that distance from the central point, which will just permit the most remote citizens to assemble as often as their public functions demand, and will include no greater number than can join in those functions: so the natural limit of a republic, is that distance from the centre, which will barely allow the representatives of the people to meet as often as may be necessary for the administration of public affairs. Can it be said, that the limits of the United States exceed this distance? It will not be said by those who recollect, that the Atlantic coast is the longest side of the Union; that, during the term of thirteen years, the representatives of the States have been almost continually assembled; and that the members, from the most distant States, are not chargeable with greater intermissions of attendance, than those from the States in the neighborhood of Congress. . . .

FAVOURABLE as this view of the subject may be, some observations remain, which will place it in a light still more satisfactory.

In the first place, it is to be remembered, that the general Government is not to be charged with the whole power of making and administering laws: its jurisdiction is limited to certain enumerated objects, which concern all the members of the republic, but which are not to be attained by the separate provisions of any. The subordinate Governments, which can extend their care to all those other objects, which can be separately provided for, will retain their due authority and activity. Were it proposed by the plan of the Convention, to abolish the Governments of the particular States, its adversaries would have some ground for their objection; though it would not be difficult to show, that if they were abolished, the general Government would be compelled, by the principle of self preservation, to reinstate them in their proper jurisdiction.

A second observation to be made is, that the immediate object of the Federal constitution, is to secure the Union of the thirteen primitive States, which we know to be practicable; and to add to them such other States, as may arise in their own bosoms, or in their neighbourhoods, which we cannot doubt to be equally practicable. The arrangement that may be necessary for those angles and fractions of our territory, which lie on our northwestern frontier, must be left to those whom further discoveries and experience will render more equal to the task.

Let it be remarked, in the third place, that the intercourse throughout the Union will be daily facilitated by new improvements. Roads will every where be shortened, and kept in better order; accommodations for travellers will be multiplied and meliorated; an interior navigation on our eastern side, will be opened throughout, or nearly throughout, the whole extent of the Thirteen States. The communication between the western and Atlantic districts, and between different parts of each, will be rendered more and more easy, by those numerous canals, with which the beneficence of nature has intersected our country, and which art finds so little difficult to connect and complete.

A fourth, and still more important consideration, is, that as almost every State will, on one side or other, be a frontier, and will thus find, in a regard to its safety, an inducement to make some sacrifices for the sake of the general protection: so the States which lie at the greatest distance from the heart of the Union, and which of course may partake least of the ordinary circulation of its benefits, will be at the same time immediately contiguous to foreign nations, and will consequently stand, on particular occasions, in greatest need of its strength and resources. It may be inconvenient for Georgia, or the States forming our western or north-eastern borders, to send their representatives to the Seat of Government; but they would find it more so to struggle alone against an invading enemy, or even to support alone the whole expense of those precautions, which may be dictated by the neighbourhood of continual danger. If they should derive less benefit therefore from the Union in some respects, than the less distant States, they will derive greater benefit from it in other respects, and thus the proper equilibrium will be maintained throughout.

I submit to you, my fellow citizens, these considerations, in full confidence that the good sense which has so often marked your decisions, will allow them their due weight and effect; and that you will never suffer difficulties, however formidable in appearance, or however fashionable the error on which they may be founded, to drive you into the gloomy and perilous scenes into which the advocates for disunion would conduct you.

No. 37.—BY JAMES MADISON

Concerning the difficulties which the Convention must have experienced in the formation of a proper plan.

AMONG the difficulties encountered by the Convention, a very important one must have lain, in combining the requisite stability and energy in government, with the inviolable attention due to liberty, and to the republican form. Without substantially accomplishing this part of their undertaking, they would have very imperfectly fulfilled the object of their appointment, or the expectation of the public: yet, that it could not be easily accomplished, will be denied by no one who is unwilling to betray his ignorance of the subject. Energy in government, is essential to that security against external and internal danger, and to that prompt and salutary execution of the laws, which enter into the very definition of good government.

Stability in government is essential to national character, and to the advantages annexed to it, as well as to that repose and confidence in the minds of the people, which are among the chief blessings of civil society. An irregular and mutable legislation is not more an evil in itself, than it is odious to the people; and it may be pronounced with assurance, that the people of this country, enlightened as they are, with regard to the nature, and interested, as the great body of them are, in the effects of good government, will never be satisfied, till some remedy be applied to the vicissitudes and uncertainties, which characterize the State administrations. On comparing, however, these valuable ingredients with the vital principles of liberty, we must perceive at once, the difficulty of mingling them together in their due proportions. . . .

How far the Convention may have succeeded in this part of their work, will better appear on a more accurate view of it. From the cursory view here taken, it must clearly appear to have been an arduous part.

Not less arduous must have been the task of making the proper line of partition, between the authority of the General, and that of the State governments. Every man will be sensible of this difficulty, in proportion as he has been accustomed to contemplate and discriminate objects, extensive and complicated in their nature. The faculties of the mind itself have never yet been distinguished and defined, with satisfactory precision, by all the efforts of the most acute and metaphysical philosophers. Sense, perception, judgment, desire, volition, memory, imagination, are found to be separated, by such delicate shades and minute gradations, that their boundaries have eluded the most subtle investigations, and remain a pregnant source of ingenious disquisition and controversy. The boundaries between the great kingdoms of nature, and still more, between the various provinces, and lesser portions, into which they are subdivided, afford another illustration of the same important truth. The most sagacious and laborious naturalists have never yet succeeded, in tracing with certainty the line which separates the district of vegetable life, from the neighboring region of unorganized matter, or which marks the termination of the former, and the commencement of the animal empire. A still greater obscurity lies in the distinctive characters, by which the objects in each of these great departments of nature have been arranged and assorted.

When we pass from the works of nature, in which all the delineations are perfectly accurate, and appear to be otherwise only from the imperfection of the eye which surveys them, to the institutions of man, in which the obscurity arises as well from the object itself, as from the organ by which it is contemplated; we must perceive the necessity of moderating still further our expectations and hopes from the efforts of human sagacity. Experience has instructed us, that no skill in the science of government has yet been able to discriminate and define, with sufficient certainty, its three great provinces, the legislative, executive, and judiciary; or even the privileges and powers of the different legislative branches. Questions daily occur in the course of practice, which prove the obscurity which reigns in these subjects, and which puzzle the greatest adepts in political science. . . .

To THE difficulties already mentioned, may be added the interfering pretensions of the larger and smaller States. We cannot err, in supposing that the former would contend for a participation in the Government, fully proportioned to their superior wealth and importance; and that the latter would not be less tenacious of the equality at present enjoyed by them. We may well suppose, that neither side would entirely yield to the other, and consequently that the struggle could be terminated only by compromise. It is extremely probable, also that after the ratio of representation had been adjusted, this very compromise must have produced a fresh struggle between the same parties, to give such a turn to the organization of the Government, and to the distribution of its powers, as would increase the importance of the branches, in forming which they had respectively obtained the greatest share of influence. There are features in the Constitution which warrant each of these suppositions; and as far as either of them is well founded, it shows that the Convention must have been compelled to sacrifice theoretical propriety to the force of extraneous considerations.

Nor could it have been the large and small States only, which would marshal themselves in opposition to each other on various points. Other combinations, resulting from a difference of local position and policy, must have created additional difficulties. As every State may be divided into different districts, and its citizens into different classes, which give birth to contending interests and local jealousies: so the different parts of the United States are distinguished from each other, by a variety of circumstances, which produce a like effect on a larger scale. And although this variety of interests, for reasons sufficiently explained in a former paper, may have a salutary influence on the administration of the Government when formed; yet every one must be sensible of the contrary influence, which must have been experienced in the task of forming it.

Would it be wonderful if, under the pressure of all these difficulties, the Convention should have been forced into some deviations from that artificial structure and regular symmetry, which an abstract view of the subject might lead an ingenious theorist to bestow on a constitution planned in his closet, or in his imagination? The real wonder is, that so many difficulties should have been surmounted; and surmounted with an unanimity almost as unprecedented, as it must have been unexpected.